living ROI

Realize, Own and Ignite Your Life

A Weekly Guide for Soulful Living

the journal

this journal belongs to:

_____

Join the community at **LivingROI.com** for support and additional resources.

connect with us

/livingroi   /livingroi   @livingroi   @livingroi

First edition ©2017 by Barbara Fagan-Smith. All rights reserved.
Feel free to share with others. This content is intended to support as many people as possible.
ISBN 978-0-692-91676-6

dedication

This journal is dedicated to my beautiful family—my husband Colin and our two daughters, Emerald and Marina. You are my inspiration.

acknowledgments

Thank you to all of the teachers who have helped me live my best life. Your lessons are infused in my consciousness and this journal. Oprah Winfrey; Tony Robbins; Jim Rohn; Louise Hay; Maya Angelou; Eckhart Tolle; Florence Scovel Shinn; Peter and Briana Borton; Richard Branson; Brian Tracy; Scott Dunsmore; Darren Hardy; Robert Kiyosaki; Hal Elrod; Henriette Anne Klauser; Michael Hyatt; Dr. Christiane Northrup, M.D.; Anthony E. Wolf, Ph.D.; Andrew Weil, M.D.; John Pollack; Michael Lynberg; Roger D'Aprix; Cheryl Richardson; Elizabeth Gilbert; David Allen; Michael Crowley; Ellen Domb; Stephen Covey; Vicki Robin; Joe Dominguez; Marie Kondo; Dale Carnegie; John Muir; Rumi; the Dalai Lama; Deepak Chopra, M.D.; Lao Tzu; Gary Zukav; David Schwartz, Ph.D.; Victor Frankl; Jeff Sanders; Jim Loehr; Tony Schwartz; Napoleon Hill; the 12-step philosophy; and all the many spiritual teachers throughout time. And to the many others who are not top of my consciousness right now.

I'd also like to acknowledge all the people who helped me actually bring this journal and the Living ROI work to fruition: my family (Colin Smith, Emerald Smith and Marina Smith); my parents (David and Patricia Fagan); my brothers and sisters (Andrew Fagan, Mairead Owens, Brian Fagan, Moira Fagan Simpson and Kathleen Fagan McCusker); my dear friends (Jo Fleming, Jennifer Rubin and Leslye Alexander); my team at ROI Communication (Ginny Henzi, Melanie Barna, Mark Briggs, John Kidon, Denise Rotman, Laura LeBleu, Kristin Durham, Lesli Gee, Sheryl Lewis, Tina Cox, JoAnn Webster, Erin Hosilyk, Allison Renda, Spencer Bullock, Barbara Baill, Clark Foy, Leslie Hess, Samantha Manss, April Green, Molly Souksamlane, Eileen Gillette, Jackie West and the late Eric Bemberess); my team at Living ROI (Karen Crocker Snell, Naomi Ture, Ric Grover, Federico Marchetti, Chelsea Smith and Leslie O. Estrada); and my coaches (Sharon Day and Marilyn Horowitz).

contents

1 introduction
2 tips for living roi
3 yearly practice
   4 About me
   5 What really matters to me
   6 Me in 5 years
   8 Gap between today and my 5-year vision
   9 My goals for the year
  10 My actions
  11 My vision board
  12 My reflections
  13 My habits
15 weekly practice
  16 Weekly practice guidance
  18 My quarter
  20 My week (13 forms for 3 months)
  72 My quarter
  74 My week (13 forms for 3 months)
126 my 6-month review
127 notes and reflections
136 about living roi
138 about barbara fagan-smith

introduction

Welcome to the Living ROI Guide for Soulful Living!
This journal will help you realize, own and ignite your life,
one week at a time.

My name is Barbara Fagan-Smith. I'm an entrepreneur, CEO and author. And I've spent many years in the pursuit of living a soulful life.

I started my professional career 30 years ago as a journalist. While based in London, I covered the revolutions in Eastern Europe and the first Gulf War. After a brief sojourn running a business in Spain, I returned to the U.S. and worked as a corporate communications professional for a Fortune 500 company. Sixteen years ago, I started my own consulting firm, working with the largest organizations in the world. Today, that business is a multimillion-dollar corporation. I was able to achieve professional success and financial freedom while maintaining a healthy and happy personal and family life. But it hasn't always been this way.

There was a time when I would work a full day, rush home, give my husband and daughters a quick kiss, then open my laptop and keep working. As the girls grew up, there were too many times I wasn't there when I wanted to be. When I look back on those days, it's scary to realize how close I came to throwing away my marriage and hurting the beautiful family we created together.

In Japanese, there is a word for death from overworking: "Karoshi."

Through that pain, I changed my life by studying and practicing multiple approaches to professional and personal development. I read hundreds of books, attended seminars and honed what I learned over time. I have synthesized my knowledge into a simple and effective weekly practice that transformed my life and allows me to live in a way that is both successful and soulful.

I created Living ROI to share what I've learned with anyone in search of a life that is more authentic, joyful and fulfilling. Because a great life doesn't just happen; it is planned. And the price of letting life happen to you, versus making life happen, is high. This journal is your roadmap to reinvention. It provides a powerful—and practical—approach to living your best life. It will help you discover and articulate the things that matter most, and create a clear path of action to achieve your most soulful life.

This journal is all about you—your hopes and goals, your needs and dreams. I encourage you to jump into this practice today. Your life is waiting!

Barbara

Barbara Fagan-Smith
Founder and Chief Catalyst, Living ROI

tips for living roi

The most important element to this practice is that you actually spend some time doing it, ideally each week. Consistency is the key. It won't be perfect. It will never be "done." It's always a work in progress. But after spending more than 20 years studying the art and science of visioning, planning and soulful living, there are a few fundamentals I've learned that I recommend you follow.

1. **Together is better:** Find one or two kindred spirits to join you
2. **Sacred time:** Schedule time on a weekly basis for planning
3. **Consistency matters:** Follow a consistent and simple practice

together is better

Identify one or two people to join you. It could be your partner, a family member or friends. Enlist people who also have a desire to live a great life and who don't want to just hope for the best and let life happen to them. Teaming up takes this practice to the next level—making it more fun, strengthening your commitment and creating a soulful experience in itself!

If you don't have a partner for this practice, it's OK to strike out on your own to start. You can tap into the Living ROI community for support, and eventually you will find your people.

> "For several years, I have been part of a group we call 'W3.' We are three entrepreneurs and mothers who meet weekly and follow this practice. We check in with each other, plan our week and support each other. As a result, we have built a deep bond and support structure that has enriched all of our lives in countless ways."
> — BARBARA

sacred time

Schedule the time on your calendar for planning.

> **Yearly:** 3 to 4 hours to complete the yearly practice (whenever you start this journal!)

> **Weekly:** 1 to 2 hours (end or beginning of each week)

consistency matters

It's important to honor the time you create to do this practice regularly. This journal is designed to give you a clear roadmap. I guarantee that if you follow this process consistently, you will have more time, get more done and live a happier and more soulful life.

yearly practice

Set the stage for your soulful life by defining who you are and what matters to you.

This part of the journal will help you identify and articulate the goals that will serve as the foundation for your weekly practice.

tips
> Find a comfortable space to work. You may find it helpful to work outside of your home, away from potential distractions.

> Don't worry about being perfect. Your answers will likely evolve over time. Just write what comes to mind today.

> Check out LivingROI.com for step-by-step support and guidance.

> *I was once afraid of people saying, 'Who does she think she is?'
> Now I have the courage to stand and say, 'This is who I am.'*
> OPRAH WINFREY

Define your important views and perspectives on your life and yourself. *tip*: Answer these in whatever way comes to you right now. You can add to it or change it later if you want.

purpose (The difference you intend to make in the world)
e.g., Help people live their best lives; be a loving and supportive wife, mother, friend, sister and daughter.

_____
_____
_____
_____

identity (Who you are and what you stand for)
e.g., I'm an entrepreneur and a catalyst. I help bring out the best in others. I create opportunity.

_____
_____
_____
_____

code of conduct (The standards you hold yourself to each day, no matter what happens)
e.g., Honesty, integrity, kindness.

_____
_____
_____
_____

values (What's most important to you)
e.g., Health, family, education, giving back.

_____
_____
_____
_____

what really matters to me
(clarity and focus)

> *The key to success is to focus our conscious mind on things we desire, not things we fear.*
> BRIAN TRACY

What is NOT working in your life right now?

_____
_____
_____
_____
_____
_____

Imagine you only have six months to live. You will be healthy for those six months. What would you do and with whom?

_____
_____
_____
_____
_____
_____
_____
_____
_____
_____
_____
_____
_____
_____

me in 5 years (my unique vision)

> *There are those who work all day, those who dream all day and those who spend an hour dreaming before setting to work to fulfill those dreams. Go into the third category because there's virtually no competition.*
> STEVEN J. ROSS

Imagine it is five years from now, and you are very happy with your life. What does it look like? Where are you? Who is with you? What are you doing? How are you spending your time? Think about your ideal life in five years in each of these areas. *tip:* Write in the present tense, as if it's already five years from now and you are living your ideal life.

personal health

_____

_____

physical space (Where you live, what your home is like, your office, your car, etc.)

_____

_____

primary relationship

_____

_____

_____

family

_____

_____

_____

making a difference (Community connection and service)

_____

_____

_____

friends and social life

spiritual connection

work/school

financial

day to day living

personal enrichment (Hobbies, classes, books, seminars)

important events and travel

important people in my life

gap between today and my 5 year vision

It's time to determine how far you are today from your five-year vision. For each topic area, estimate on a scale of zero to 10 how close you already are to your vision; zero means you're very far away today from where you want to be, and 10 means your vision is already a reality.

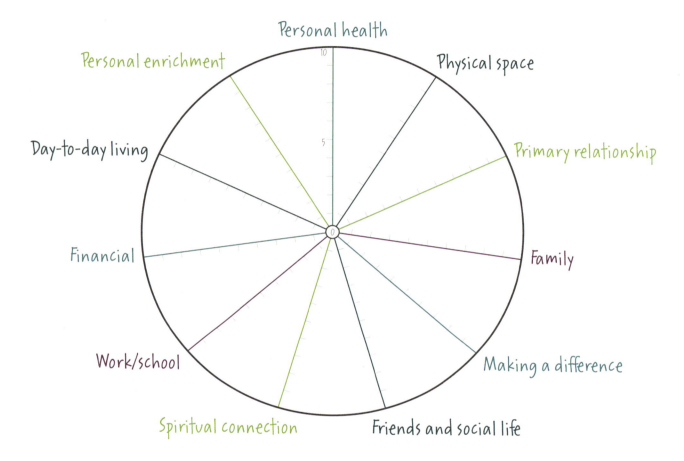

Shade in the area that represents the gap. This area is the opportunity you're going to realize over the coming weeks, months and years. It gives you a clear picture of what needs to be done to make your vision a reality.

# my goals for the year

" The key is not to prioritize what's on your schedule, but to schedule your priorities. "
STEPHEN COVEY

Based on your vision, identify your top goals for the year.

tips
> After years of experience, I have learned that it is ideal to have your #1 goal be about your own wellbeing and your #2 goal be about your primary relationship and family.

> Write your goals in the current tense, not the future tense (just as you did with your vision). Your brain doesn't know the difference, and you will automatically move towards what you say already exists! This works like magic, but it is actually based in science. The reticular activating system in your brain (responsible for regulating alertness and attention) is programmed by what you focus on, and it naturally moves you towards your vision and goals.

> Make the titles of your goals personal and relevant to help you remember them. For instance: Rocking Relationship with [partner's name], Cozy Home, Peak Health, Supportive Parent, Dynamite Dancer, Outrageous Adventurer, Financial Genius, Fitness Guru. Have some fun with this!

#1 Wellbeing
_____
_____

#2 Primary relationship and family
_____
_____

#3 _____
_____

#4 _____
_____

#5 _____
_____

#6 _____
_____

my actions

> *" A goal without a plan is just a wish. "*
> ANTOINE DE SAINT-EXUPÉRY

Write down all of the actions you can take to achieve each goal. Identify the first few logical actions for each of your goals and schedule when you will do them.

goal	actions	by when
#1 Wellbeing		
#2 Primary relationship and family		
#3		
#4		
#5		
#6		

my vision board

" *Envisioning the end is enough to put the means in motion.* "

DOROTHEA BRANDE

Create your individual and/or your family vision board. Find or draw images that represent elements of your goals and create a montage of pictures on paper or on the computer. *tip:* You can find images by searching on the internet, cutting out images from magazines and/or drawing images. You may want to include key words as part of your montage so it's easy for you to remember your vision.

Here is a sample vision board:

my reflections

" Success is something you attract by the person you become. "
JIM ROHN

Who do you need to become to live the life you want to live?

What are the traits of people you admire?

What do I want to be more of?

Identify traits and actions to strengthen and build yourself and your character.

traits	actions
A reader	
A listener	
A networker	
More patient	
More caring	
More thoughtful	
More grateful	
More authentic	
More responsible	
More generous	
More resilient	
More persistent	

 my habits

Determine what rhythm you want in your life daily and weekly. Here are some ideas.

habit/practice	notes on when and how
Meditation/silence (when and for how long)	
Exercise (what type and when)	
Journaling (when)	
Gratitude practice (think of all the things you are grateful for in the moment)	
Visualization practice (picture your vision and goals for your life coming true)	
Review your day (take time at the end of your day to reflect)	
Sleep (how much and when)	
Healthy eating	
Letter/card writing (how frequently)	
Reading (how much and when)	
Making love (how frequently)	
Time with friends (with whom and when)	
Being creative (art, music, etc.—what and when)	
Cook (when and how frequently)	
Play (what and when)	
Date (with partner, children, friends, etc.)	
Self-Care (massage, sauna, other body work—what and how frequently)	
Weekly practice (this journal)	

Add any others that you want to include but aren't on the list and incorporate them into your life each week.

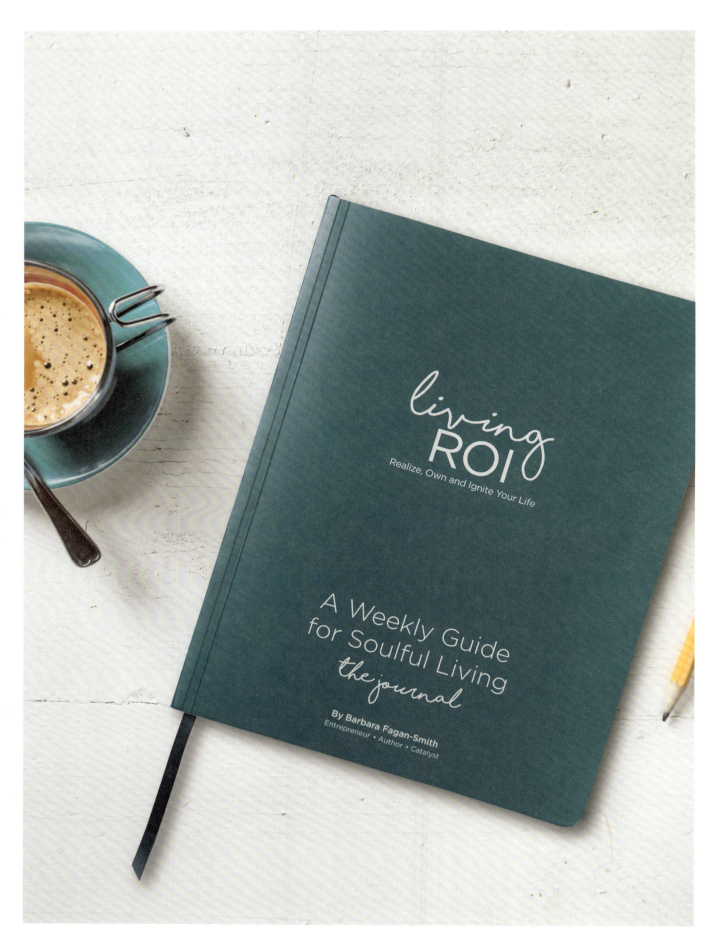

weekly practice

The weekly practice is the heart of Living ROI. Taking consistent action makes the difference between life happening to you, versus you making life happen. This is your life—each week, each day, each moment. This is where your soulful life is born.

This section includes 26 "my week" forms and two "my quarter" forms—six months of weekly practice.

how to complete "my week" practice

The first step in the weekly practice is to fill out the **my quarter** form at the start of each quarter to look back at what you've accomplished during the last three months, and to look forward at the events and projects coming up for the next three months. Once you've completed your weekly practice for a full quarter, it will be much easier for you to reflect back on the events, projects and accomplishments from that time. You will be amazed at what you've done. I've found, even on a weekly basis, people forget what they've accomplished, and that's why looking back, acknowledging and celebrating, is part of this practice. In the **my quarter** process, you will also identify what specific actions you're going to take towards your goals during the quarter.

W3 group—Jennifer, Barbara and Jo—doing their weekly practice.

The most important part of this journal is the weekly practice. For several years, I have been part of a group we call "W3." We are three entrepreneurs and mothers who meet weekly and follow this practice. This is how we structure our weekly get-togethers:

We get together each Sunday afternoon at one of our homes or in a café or restaurant.

We spend about 30 minutes catching up and checking in.

We set a timer—on a phone—for 30 minutes and fill out our weekly plan.

We set a timer for 10 minutes each and share our plans for the week.

This process takes one to two hours, depending on how much time we take to check in before we start working on our weekly plan. You could do it in one hour if you get straight to it and skip the check-in. And if you're working on your own, you can get it done in 30 minutes; however, I strongly recommend doing it with a partner or two.

The first action each week is to remind yourself what your **top goals for the year** are. That keeps them front and center as you plan your week. Next, you get to **celebrate last week** and acknowledge all that you accomplished, big and small. I know for a fact that you did more than you can remember off the top of your head. Use your calendar, your email, your journal and even your social media posts to help you remember.

The next step is to think about what your **best week** would look like. What are the most important things that can happen to make this a great week?

In the **my habits** section, you get to identify which habits you will focus on this week and how often. You can actually fill in which days you plan to do each habit, or you can just indicate how many days that week you will do it. At the end of the week, add up what you actually did. I've never been 100% on these habits, and often I adjust my expectations week to week based on my schedule. You can change up habits. Sometimes a habit becomes so ingrained that you don't need to write it down anymore, and you can add something new.

In the **my activities and actions for the week** section, you'll get into the detail of each day. Identify the big uses of your time—meetings, events, exercise, travel. From a very practical perspective, this is an opportunity to make sure you're not double-booked, and ensure that you're prepared for what's coming up in the week. There is a place for you to list your **morning rituals** and **evening rituals**—how you want to start and end your days this week. There is also space to identify a few things that are **just for you**—those activities that really feed your soul—that you will fit into this week. In the **inspiration** section, you can list quotes, thoughts, books, songs or stories that inspired you last week and inspirational content that you will seek out this week.

As you do this practice—looking at your calendar and thinking about what is coming up for your week—you will inevitably identify **other tasks and ideas to capture**, so we've created a weekly page for that. In addition, there's a page for **notes and reflections** for each week.

Once you've completed your weekly practice, you can update your digital and physical calendars. Also, communicate key activities with those who might be impacted—your family, friends and coworkers. Will you be home late one day? Will you be traveling? Is there an event you need to let others know about? I've found there are fewer surprises and more delights in my week when I do this. Through this weekly practice, you get to see if you're spending your time, day-to-day, in a way that aligns with your vision and goals for your life. And if you're not, this is your opportunity to change it.

my quarter of _____

Reflect back on your important events, travel and projects over the last quarter:

month 1:	month 2:	month 3:

Identify your important events, travel and projects coming up:

month 1:	month 2:	month 3:

Actions you plan to take each month for your goals:

month 1:	month 2:	month 3:

notes and reflections

 my week of _____

top goals for the year (Reminder from page 9)

_____   _____
_____   _____
_____   _____

celebrate last week Accomplishments, special moments and inspiration
Look back on your week and take note of important events and special moments. Did you make progress on your goals?

_____   _____
_____   _____
_____   _____

my best week
Imagine this coming week has been super successful. What will you have done?

_____   _____
_____   _____
_____   _____

my habits
What habits do you want to practice this week? Set the number of times you want to do each habit this week, and then keep track of what you actually do.

HABIT	MON	TUE	WED	THU	FRI	SAT	SUN	# GOAL	# ACTUAL
								TOTAL	

my activities and actions for the week

Capture your important activities and actions for the week. Add these to your personal calendar.

MONDAY

TUESDAY

WEDNESDAY

THURSDAY

FRIDAY

SATURDAY

SUNDAY

MORNING RITUALS

EVENING RITUALS

JUST FOR YOU

INSPIRATION

other tasks and ideas i want to capture

notes and reflections

 my week of _____

top goals for the year (Reminder from page 9)

_____   _____
_____   _____
_____   _____

celebrate last week Accomplishments, special moments and inspiration

Look back on your week and take note of important events and special moments. Did you make progress on your goals?

_____   _____
_____   _____
_____   _____
_____   _____

my best week

Imagine this coming week has been super successful. What will you have done?

_____   _____
_____   _____
_____   _____
_____   _____

my habits

What habits do you want to practice this week? Set the number of times you want to do each habit this week, and then keep track of what you actually do.

HABIT	MON	TUE	WED	THU	FRI	SAT	SUN	# GOAL	# ACTUAL
								TOTAL	

my activities and actions for the week

Capture your important activities and actions for the week. Add these to your personal calendar.

MONDAY

TUESDAY

WEDNESDAY

THURSDAY

FRIDAY

SATURDAY

SUNDAY

MORNING RITUALS

EVENING RITUALS

JUST FOR YOU

INSPIRATION

other tasks and ideas i want to capture

 notes and reflections

 my week of _____

top goals for the year (Reminder from page 9)

_____ _____
_____ _____
_____ _____

celebrate last week Accomplishments, special moments and inspiration

Look back on your week and take note of important events and special moments. Did you make progress on your goals?

_____ _____
_____ _____
_____ _____
_____ _____

my best week

Imagine this coming week has been super successful. What will you have done?

_____ _____
_____ _____
_____ _____
_____ _____

my habits

What habits do you want to practice this week? Set the number of times you want to do each habit this week, and then keep track of what you actually do.

HABIT	MON	TUE	WED	THU	FRI	SAT	SUN	# GOAL	# ACTUAL
								TOTAL	

my activities and actions for the week

Capture your important activities and actions for the week. Add these to your personal calendar.

MONDAY

TUESDAY

WEDNESDAY

THURSDAY

FRIDAY

SATURDAY

SUNDAY

MORNING RITUALS

EVENING RITUALS

JUST FOR YOU

INSPIRATION

other tasks and ideas i want to capture

notes and reflections

 my week of _____

top goals for the year (Reminder from page 9)

_____   _____
_____   _____
_____   _____

celebrate last week Accomplishments, special moments and inspiration
Look back on your week and take note of important events and special moments. Did you make progress on your goals?

_____   _____
_____   _____
_____   _____
_____   _____

my best week
Imagine this coming week has been super successful. What will you have done?

_____   _____
_____   _____
_____   _____
_____   _____

my habits
What habits do you want to practice this week? Set the number of times you want to do each habit this week, and then keep track of what you actually do.

HABIT	MON	TUE	WED	THU	FRI	SAT	SUN	# GOAL	# ACTUAL
								TOTAL	

my activities and actions for the week

Capture your important activities and actions for the week. Add these to your personal calendar.

MONDAY

TUESDAY

WEDNESDAY

THURSDAY

FRIDAY

SATURDAY

SUNDAY

MORNING RITUALS

EVENING RITUALS

JUST FOR YOU

INSPIRATION

other tasks and ideas i want to capture

 my week of _____

top goals for the year (Reminder from page 9)

_____ _____
_____ _____
_____ _____

celebrate last week Accomplishments, special moments and inspiration

Look back on your week and take note of important events and special moments. Did you make progress on your goals?

_____ _____
_____ _____
_____ _____
_____ _____

my best week

Imagine this coming week has been super successful. What will you have done?

_____ _____
_____ _____
_____ _____
_____ _____

my habits

What habits do you want to practice this week? Set the number of times you want to do each habit this week, and then keep track of what you actually do.

HABIT	MON	TUE	WED	THU	FRI	SAT	SUN	# GOAL	# ACTUAL
								TOTAL	

# my activities and actions for the week

Capture your important activities and actions for the week. Add these to your personal calendar.

MONDAY

TUESDAY

WEDNESDAY

THURSDAY

FRIDAY

SATURDAY

SUNDAY

MORNING RITUALS

EVENING RITUALS

JUST FOR YOU

INSPIRATION

other tasks and ideas i want to capture

notes and reflections

my week of _____

top goals for the year (Reminder from page 9)

_____ _____
_____ _____
_____ _____

celebrate last week Accomplishments, special moments and inspiration

Look back on your week and take note of important events and special moments. Did you make progress on your goals?

_____ _____
_____ _____
_____ _____
_____ _____

my best week

Imagine this coming week has been super successful. What will you have done?

_____ _____
_____ _____
_____ _____
_____ _____

my habits

What habits do you want to practice this week? Set the number of times you want to do each habit this week, and then keep track of what you actually do.

HABIT	MON	TUE	WED	THU	FRI	SAT	SUN	# GOAL	# ACTUAL
								TOTAL	

my activities and actions for the week

Capture your important activities and actions for the week. Add these to your personal calendar.

MONDAY

TUESDAY

WEDNESDAY

THURSDAY

FRIDAY

SATURDAY

SUNDAY

MORNING RITUALS

EVENING RITUALS

JUST FOR YOU

INSPIRATION

other tasks and ideas i want to capture

# notes and reflections

 my week of _____

top goals for the year (Reminder from page 9)

_____   _____
_____   _____
_____   _____

celebrate last week Accomplishments, special moments and inspiration

Look back on your week and take note of important events and special moments. Did you make progress on your goals?

_____   _____
_____   _____
_____   _____
_____   _____

my best week

Imagine this coming week has been super successful. What will you have done?

_____   _____
_____   _____
_____   _____
_____   _____

my habits

What habits do you want to practice this week? Set the number of times you want to do each habit this week, and then keep track of what you actually do.

HABIT	MON	TUE	WED	THU	FRI	SAT	SUN	# GOAL	# ACTUAL
								TOTAL	

my activities and actions for the week

Capture your important activities and actions for the week. Add these to your personal calendar.

MONDAY

TUESDAY

WEDNESDAY

THURSDAY

FRIDAY

SATURDAY

SUNDAY

MORNING RITUALS

EVENING RITUALS

JUST FOR YOU

INSPIRATION

other tasks and ideas i want to capture

notes and reflections

my week of _____

top goals for the year (Reminder from page 9)

_____
_____
_____

_____
_____
_____

celebrate last week Accomplishments, special moments and inspiration

Look back on your week and take note of important events and special moments. Did you make progress on your goals?

_____
_____
_____
_____

_____
_____
_____
_____

my best week

Imagine this coming week has been super successful. What will you have done?

_____
_____
_____
_____

_____
_____
_____
_____

my habits

What habits do you want to practice this week? Set the number of times you want to do each habit this week, and then keep track of what you actually do.

HABIT	MON	TUE	WED	THU	FRI	SAT	SUN	# GOAL	# ACTUAL
							TOTAL		

my activities and actions for the week

Capture your important activities and actions for the week. Add these to your personal calendar.

MONDAY

TUESDAY

WEDNESDAY

THURSDAY

FRIDAY

SATURDAY

SUNDAY

MORNING RITUALS

EVENING RITUALS

JUST FOR YOU

INSPIRATION

other tasks and ideas i want to capture

notes and reflections

 my week of _____

top goals for the year (Reminder from page 9)

_____ _____
_____ _____
_____ _____

celebrate last week Accomplishments, special moments and inspiration

Look back on your week and take note of important events and special moments. Did you make progress on your goals?

_____ _____
_____ _____
_____ _____

my best week

Imagine this coming week has been super successful. What will you have done?

_____ _____
_____ _____
_____ _____

my habits

What habits do you want to practice this week? Set the number of times you want to do each habit this week, and then keep track of what you actually do.

HABIT	MON	TUE	WED	THU	FRI	SAT	SUN	# GOAL	# ACTUAL
							TOTAL		

my activities and actions for the week

Capture your important activities and actions for the week. Add these to your personal calendar.

MONDAY

TUESDAY

WEDNESDAY

THURSDAY

FRIDAY

SATURDAY

SUNDAY

MORNING RITUALS

EVENING RITUALS

JUST FOR YOU

INSPIRATION

other tasks and ideas i want to capture

notes and reflections

my week of _____

top goals for the year (Reminder from page 9)

_____ _____
_____ _____
_____ _____

celebrate last week — Accomplishments, special moments and inspiration

Look back on your week and take note of important events and special moments. Did you make progress on your goals?

_____ _____
_____ _____
_____ _____
_____ _____

my best week

Imagine this coming week has been super successful. What will you have done?

_____ _____
_____ _____
_____ _____
_____ _____

my habits

What habits do you want to practice this week? Set the number of times you want to do each habit this week, and then keep track of what you actually do.

HABIT	MON	TUE	WED	THU	FRI	SAT	SUN	# GOAL	# ACTUAL
							TOTAL		

my activities and actions for the week

Capture your important activities and actions for the week. Add these to your personal calendar.

MONDAY

TUESDAY

WEDNESDAY

THURSDAY

FRIDAY

SATURDAY

SUNDAY

MORNING RITUALS

EVENING RITUALS

JUST FOR YOU

INSPIRATION

other tasks and ideas i want to capture

notes and reflections

 my week of _____

top goals for the year (Reminder from page 9)

_____   _____
_____   _____
_____   _____

celebrate last week Accomplishments, special moments and inspiration

Look back on your week and take note of important events and special moments. Did you make progress on your goals?

_____   _____
_____   _____
_____   _____
_____   _____

my best week

Imagine this coming week has been super successful. What will you have done?

_____   _____
_____   _____
_____   _____
_____   _____

my habits

What habits do you want to practice this week? Set the number of times you want to do each habit this week, and then keep track of what you actually do.

HABIT	MON	TUE	WED	THU	FRI	SAT	SUN	# GOAL	# ACTUAL
								TOTAL	

my activities and actions for the week

Capture your important activities and actions for the week. Add these to your personal calendar.

MONDAY

TUESDAY

WEDNESDAY

THURSDAY

FRIDAY

SATURDAY

SUNDAY

MORNING RITUALS

EVENING RITUALS

JUST FOR YOU

INSPIRATION

other tasks and ideas i want to capture

notes and reflections

 my week of _____

top goals for the year (Reminder from page 9)

celebrate last week Accomplishments, special moments and inspiration
Look back on your week and take note of important events and special moments. Did you make progress on your goals?

my best week
Imagine this coming week has been super successful. What will you have done?

my habits
What habits do you want to practice this week? Set the number of times you want to do each habit this week, and then keep track of what you actually do.

HABIT	MON	TUE	WED	THU	FRI	SAT	SUN	# GOAL	# ACTUAL
							TOTAL		

my activities and actions for the week

Capture your important activities and actions for the week. Add these to your personal calendar.

MONDAY

TUESDAY

WEDNESDAY

THURSDAY

FRIDAY

SATURDAY

SUNDAY

MORNING RITUALS

EVENING RITUALS

JUST FOR YOU

INSPIRATION

other tasks and ideas i want to capture

notes and reflections

 my week of _____

top goals for the year (Reminder from page 9)

_____   _____
_____   _____
_____   _____

celebrate last week Accomplishments, special moments and inspiration

Look back on your week and take note of important events and special moments. Did you make progress on your goals?

_____   _____
_____   _____
_____   _____
_____   _____

my best week

Imagine this coming week has been super successful. What will you have done?

_____   _____
_____   _____
_____   _____
_____   _____

my habits

What habits do you want to practice this week? Set the number of times you want to do each habit this week, and then keep track of what you actually do.

HABIT	MON	TUE	WED	THU	FRI	SAT	SUN	# GOAL	# ACTUAL
								TOTAL	

my activities and actions for the week

Capture your important activities and actions for the week. Add these to your personal calendar.

MONDAY

TUESDAY

WEDNESDAY

THURSDAY

FRIDAY

SATURDAY

SUNDAY

MORNING RITUALS

EVENING RITUALS

JUST FOR YOU

INSPIRATION

other tasks and ideas i want to capture

my quarter of _____

Reflect back on your important events, travel and projects over the last quarter:

month 1:	month 2:	month 3:

Identify your important events, travel and projects coming up:

month 1:	month 2:	month 3:

Actions you plan to take each month for your goals:

month 1:	month 2:	month 3:

 my week of _____

top goals for the year (Reminder from page 9)

_____   _____
_____   _____
_____   _____

celebrate last week Accomplishments, special moments and inspiration

Look back on your week and take note of important events and special moments. Did you make progress on your goals?

_____   _____
_____   _____
_____   _____
_____   _____

my best week

Imagine this coming week has been super successful. What will you have done?

_____   _____
_____   _____
_____   _____
_____   _____

my habits

What habits do you want to practice this week? Set the number of times you want to do each habit this week, and then keep track of what you actually do.

HABIT	MON	TUE	WED	THU	FRI	SAT	SUN	# GOAL	# ACTUAL
							TOTAL		

my activities and actions for the week

Capture your important activities and actions for the week. Add these to your personal calendar.

MONDAY

TUESDAY

WEDNESDAY

THURSDAY

FRIDAY

SATURDAY

SUNDAY

MORNING RITUALS   EVENING RITUALS   JUST FOR YOU   INSPIRATION

other tasks and ideas i want to capture

 my week of _____

top goals for the year (Reminder from page 9)

_____   _____
_____   _____
_____   _____

celebrate last week Accomplishments, special moments and inspiration

Look back on your week and take note of important events and special moments. Did you make progress on your goals?

_____   _____
_____   _____
_____   _____
_____   _____

my best week

Imagine this coming week has been super successful. What will you have done?

_____   _____
_____   _____
_____   _____
_____   _____

my habits

What habits do you want to practice this week? Set the number of times you want to do each habit this week, and then keep track of what you actually do.

HABIT	MON	TUE	WED	THU	FRI	SAT	SUN	# GOAL	# ACTUAL
								TOTAL	

my activities and actions for the week

Capture your important activities and actions for the week. Add these to your personal calendar.

MONDAY

TUESDAY

WEDNESDAY

THURSDAY

FRIDAY

SATURDAY

SUNDAY

MORNING RITUALS

EVENING RITUALS

JUST FOR YOU

INSPIRATION

other tasks and ideas i want to capture

my week of _____

top goals for the year (Reminder from page 9)

_____   _____
_____   _____
_____   _____

celebrate last week Accomplishments, special moments and inspiration

Look back on your week and take note of important events and special moments. Did you make progress on your goals?

_____   _____
_____   _____
_____   _____

my best week

Imagine this coming week has been super successful. What will you have done?

_____   _____
_____   _____
_____   _____

my habits

What habits do you want to practice this week? Set the number of times you want to do each habit this week, and then keep track of what you actually do.

HABIT	MON	TUE	WED	THU	FRI	SAT	SUN	# GOAL	# ACTUAL
								TOTAL	

my activities and actions for the week

Capture your important activities and actions for the week. Add these to your personal calendar.

MONDAY

TUESDAY

WEDNESDAY

THURSDAY

FRIDAY

SATURDAY

SUNDAY

MORNING RITUALS

EVENING RITUALS

JUST FOR YOU

INSPIRATION

other tasks and ideas i want to capture

notes and reflections

my week of _____

top goals for the year (Reminder from page 9)

_____   _____
_____   _____
_____   _____

celebrate last week Accomplishments, special moments and inspiration

Look back on your week and take note of important events and special moments. Did you make progress on your goals?

_____   _____
_____   _____
_____   _____
_____   _____

my best week

Imagine this coming week has been super successful. What will you have done?

_____   _____
_____   _____
_____   _____
_____   _____

my habits

What habits do you want to practice this week? Set the number of times you want to do each habit this week, and then keep track of what you actually do.

HABIT	MON	TUE	WED	THU	FRI	SAT	SUN	# GOAL	# ACTUAL
									TOTAL

my activities and actions for the week

Capture your important activities and actions for the week. Add these to your personal calendar.

MONDAY

TUESDAY

WEDNESDAY

THURSDAY

FRIDAY

SATURDAY

SUNDAY

MORNING RITUALS

EVENING RITUALS

JUST FOR YOU

INSPIRATION

other tasks and ideas i want to capture

my week of _____

top goals for the year (Reminder from page 9)

celebrate last week Accomplishments, special moments and inspiration
Look back on your week and take note of important events and special moments. Did you make progress on your goals?

my best week
Imagine this coming week has been super successful. What will you have done?

my habits
What habits do you want to practice this week? Set the number of times you want to do each habit this week, and then keep track of what you actually do.

HABIT	MON	TUE	WED	THU	FRI	SAT	SUN	# GOAL	# ACTUAL
								TOTAL	

my activities and actions for the week

Capture your important activities and actions for the week. Add these to your personal calendar.

MONDAY

TUESDAY

WEDNESDAY

THURSDAY

FRIDAY

SATURDAY

SUNDAY

MORNING RITUALS

EVENING RITUALS

JUST FOR YOU

INSPIRATION

other tasks and ideas i want to capture

 notes and reflections

 my week of _____

top goals for the year (Reminder from page 9)

_____ _____
_____ _____
_____ _____

celebrate last week Accomplishments, special moments and inspiration

Look back on your week and take note of important events and special moments. Did you make progress on your goals?

_____ _____
_____ _____
_____ _____
_____ _____

my best week

Imagine this coming week has been super successful. What will you have done?

_____ _____
_____ _____
_____ _____
_____ _____

my habits

What habits do you want to practice this week? Set the number of times you want to do each habit this week, and then keep track of what you actually do.

HABIT	MON	TUE	WED	THU	FRI	SAT	SUN	# GOAL	# ACTUAL
							TOTAL		

my activities and actions for the week

Capture your important activities and actions for the week. Add these to your personal calendar.

MONDAY

TUESDAY

WEDNESDAY

THURSDAY

FRIDAY

SATURDAY

SUNDAY

MORNING RITUALS

EVENING RITUALS

JUST FOR YOU

INSPIRATION

other tasks and ideas i want to capture

my week of _____

top goals for the year (Reminder from page 9)

_____   _____
_____   _____
_____   _____

celebrate last week Accomplishments, special moments and inspiration

Look back on your week and take note of important events and special moments. Did you make progress on your goals?

_____   _____
_____   _____
_____   _____
_____   _____
_____   _____

my best week

Imagine this coming week has been super successful. What will you have done?

_____   _____
_____   _____
_____   _____
_____   _____

my habits

What habits do you want to practice this week? Set the number of times you want to do each habit this week, and then keep track of what you actually do.

HABIT	MON	TUE	WED	THU	FRI	SAT	SUN	# GOAL	# ACTUAL
									TOTAL

my activities and actions for the week

Capture your important activities and actions for the week. Add these to your personal calendar.

MONDAY

TUESDAY

WEDNESDAY

THURSDAY

FRIDAY

SATURDAY

SUNDAY

MORNING RITUALS

EVENING RITUALS

JUST FOR YOU

INSPIRATION

other tasks and ideas i want to capture

 notes and reflections

my week of _____

top goals for the year (Reminder from page 9)

_____ _____
_____ _____
_____ _____

celebrate last week Accomplishments, special moments and inspiration

Look back on your week and take note of important events and special moments. Did you make progress on your goals?

_____ _____
_____ _____
_____ _____
_____ _____

my best week

Imagine this coming week has been super successful. What will you have done?

_____ _____
_____ _____
_____ _____
_____ _____

my habits

What habits do you want to practice this week? Set the number of times you want to do each habit this week, and then keep track of what you actually do.

HABIT	MON	TUE	WED	THU	FRI	SAT	SUN	# GOAL	# ACTUAL
							TOTAL		

my activities and actions for the week

Capture your important activities and actions for the week. Add these to your personal calendar.

MONDAY

TUESDAY

WEDNESDAY

THURSDAY

FRIDAY

SATURDAY

SUNDAY

MORNING RITUALS

EVENING RITUALS

JUST FOR YOU

INSPIRATION

other tasks and ideas i want to capture

notes and reflections

 my week of _____

top goals for the year (Reminder from page 9)

_____ _____
_____ _____
_____ _____

celebrate last week Accomplishments, special moments and inspiration

Look back on your week and take note of important events and special moments. Did you make progress on your goals?

_____ _____
_____ _____
_____ _____
_____ _____

my best week

Imagine this coming week has been super successful. What will you have done?

_____ _____
_____ _____
_____ _____
_____ _____

my habits

What habits do you want to practice this week? Set the number of times you want to do each habit this week, and then keep track of what you actually do.

HABIT	MON	TUE	WED	THU	FRI	SAT	SUN	# GOAL	# ACTUAL
								TOTAL	

 *my activities and actions for the week*

Capture your important activities and actions for the week. Add these to your personal calendar.

MONDAY

TUESDAY

WEDNESDAY

THURSDAY

FRIDAY

SATURDAY

SUNDAY

MORNING RITUALS

EVENING RITUALS

JUST FOR YOU

INSPIRATION

other tasks and ideas i want to capture

my week of _____

top goals for the year (Reminder from page 9)

_____   _____
_____   _____

celebrate last week Accomplishments, special moments and inspiration

Look back on your week and take note of important events and special moments. Did you make progress on your goals?

_____   _____
_____   _____
_____   _____

my best week

Imagine this coming week has been super successful. What will you have done?

_____   _____
_____   _____
_____   _____

my habits

What habits do you want to practice this week? Set the number of times you want to do each habit this week, and then keep track of what you actually do.

HABIT	MON	TUE	WED	THU	FRI	SAT	SUN	# GOAL	# ACTUAL
								TOTAL	

my activities and actions for the week

Capture your important activities and actions for the week. Add these to your personal calendar.

MONDAY

TUESDAY

WEDNESDAY

THURSDAY

FRIDAY

SATURDAY

SUNDAY

MORNING RITUALS	EVENING RITUALS	JUST FOR YOU	INSPIRATION

other tasks and ideas i want to capture

# notes and reflections

my week of _____

top goals for the year (Reminder from page 9)

_____   _____
_____   _____
_____   _____

celebrate last week Accomplishments, special moments and inspiration

Look back on your week and take note of important events and special moments. Did you make progress on your goals?

_____   _____
_____   _____
_____   _____
_____   _____

my best week

Imagine this coming week has been super successful. What will you have done?

_____   _____
_____   _____
_____   _____
_____   _____

my habits

What habits do you want to practice this week? Set the number of times you want to do each habit this week, and then keep track of what you actually do.

HABIT	MON	TUE	WED	THU	FRI	SAT	SUN	# GOAL	# ACTUAL
								TOTAL	

Capture your important activities and actions for the week. Add these to your personal calendar.

MONDAY

TUESDAY

WEDNESDAY

THURSDAY

FRIDAY

SATURDAY

SUNDAY

MORNING RITUALS

EVENING RITUALS

JUST FOR YOU

INSPIRATION

other tasks and ideas i want to capture

my week of _____

top goals for the year (Reminder from page 9)

_____   _____
_____   _____

celebrate last week   Accomplishments, special moments and inspiration

Look back on your week and take note of important events and special moments. Did you make progress on your goals?

_____   _____
_____   _____
_____   _____

my best week

Imagine this coming week has been super successful. What will you have done?

_____   _____
_____   _____
_____   _____

my habits

What habits do you want to practice this week? Set the number of times you want to do each habit this week, and then keep track of what you actually do.

HABIT	MON	TUE	WED	THU	FRI	SAT	SUN	# GOAL	# ACTUAL
								TOTAL	

my activities and actions for the week

Capture your important activities and actions for the week. Add these to your personal calendar.

MONDAY

TUESDAY

WEDNESDAY

THURSDAY

FRIDAY

SATURDAY

SUNDAY

MORNING RITUALS	EVENING RITUALS	JUST FOR YOU	INSPIRATION

other tasks and ideas i want to capture

# notes and reflections

my week of _____

top goals for the year (Reminder from page 9)

_____   _____
_____   _____
_____   _____

celebrate last week Accomplishments, special moments and inspiration

Look back on your week and take note of important events and special moments. Did you make progress on your goals?

_____   _____
_____   _____
_____   _____
_____   _____

my best week

Imagine this coming week has been super successful. What will you have done?

_____   _____
_____   _____
_____   _____
_____   _____

my habits

What habits do you want to practice this week? Set the number of times you want to do each habit this week, and then keep track of what you actually do.

HABIT	MON	TUE	WED	THU	FRI	SAT	SUN	# GOAL	# ACTUAL
								TOTAL	

my activities and actions for the week

Capture your important activities and actions for the week. Add these to your personal calendar.

MONDAY

TUESDAY

WEDNESDAY

THURSDAY

FRIDAY

SATURDAY

SUNDAY

MORNING RITUALS

EVENING RITUALS

JUST FOR YOU

INSPIRATION

other tasks and ideas i want to capture

# my 6-month review

Now that you've completed your first six months of this practice, take some time to review your progress and goals and make adjustments as needed for the next six months.

What were your greatest accomplishments, big and small, during the last six months?

_____
_____
_____
_____
_____
_____
_____
_____

In reviewing your goals, is there anything you found that needs to be added or changed?

_____
_____
_____
_____
_____
_____
_____
_____

What are the most important things you need to accomplish, big and small, to make the next six months successful and soulful?

_____
_____
_____
_____
_____
_____
_____
_____

notes and reflections

 notes and reflections

notes and reflections

notes and reflections

 notes and reflections

notes and reflections

about living roi

At Living ROI, we are dedicated to helping you live a soulful life—one that is authentic, rewarding and joyful. Barbara Fagan-Smith created Living ROI to share her insights and help people realize, own and ignite their lives, one week at a time.

The practice of weekly planning is at the heart of Living ROI. This journal is designed to help you acknowledge your life today, envision your best tomorrow and take the action you need to live a happier and fuller life.

You can build upon your journal activity at LivingROI.com, where you'll find workshops, videos and techniques for honing your weekly practice, as well as a chance to connect with a community of others seeking a more soulful life.

about barbara fagan-smith

Barbara Fagan-Smith is passionate about helping people live their best lives—personally and professionally.

An entrepreneur and author, Barbara is the founder and Chief Catalyst of Living ROI, the founder and CEO of ROI Communication and the founder of the non-profit foundation Family ROI. Her newest venture is Living ROI, which she began with the ambition of helping as many people as she can live fuller and more meaningful lives.

ROI Communication is the largest independent consulting firm focused exclusively on employee communication and engagement at global Fortune 500 companies. By strengthening communication within organizations, employees are inspired to collaborate better, contribute more and become stronger advocates of their business, culture and brand.

Family ROI is a non-profit foundation dedicated to helping people of all backgrounds apply proven business principles to revitalize, focus and strengthen the most important organization in the world—their own family. Barbara is the author of *The Family ROI Experience: A Step-by-Step Guide to Realizing your Best Family*.

Before beginning her business career, Barbara worked as a London-based television producer for ABC News, where she covered the revolutions in Eastern Europe and the 1991 Gulf War for ABC News *PrimeTime Live* and *World News Tonight*. Earlier, she covered international business and produced national radio programs for ABC. She earned a Bachelor of Arts in Journalism and Communications from Humboldt State University.

Barbara was named one of Silicon Valley's most influential women by the *Silicon Valley Business Journal*. She was also selected as a winner of the Enterprising Women of the Year Awards, an annual tribute to North America's top women entrepreneurs.

Barbara has been married to Colin Smith for 25 years, and they have two daughters, Emerald and Marina. Barbara and her family live in Santa Cruz, California, with their peacock Mango and the neighborhood cows across the street.

Printed on FSC-certified paper containing 30% post-consumer fiber.